R. H. C. Davis'

A HISTORY OF MEDIEVAL EUROPE

From Constantine to Saint Louis

Student Guide

Dustin Warren

MEMORIA PRESS

MEMORIA PRESS
www.MemoriaPress.com

R. H. C. Davis'
A HISTORY OF MEDIEVAL EUROPE
From Constantine to Saint Louis

STUDENT GUIDE
Dustin Warren

ISBN 978-1-5477-0252-7

First Edition © 2020 Memoria Press

Cover Illustration: Edmund Blair Leighton

CONTENTS

INTRODUCTION

Students often see history as a boring topic—a set of dates, events, and people that must be painstakingly memorized. History *is* a set of dates, events, and people, but these are only the parts of history, as setting, plot, and characters are parts of a story. In fact, the Greek word *historia*, from which we get history, means "narrative." History, then, is a story. Everyone loves stories. They are essential to our human nature. We need not search for proof of this. Throughout the ages, humans have told stories of themselves, both to delight and to instruct. And to guide His people, God Himself employed this means, as evidenced by the Bible's clear emphasis on narrative—*historia.* So as you lead your student(s) through *A History of Medieval Europe,* remember that the most important part of what you teach is not just a date, an event, or a person. You are helping them to discover a story, even *their* story. The Middle Ages are stereotyped by their nickname: the Dark Ages. However, the period was anything but dark. There was indeed plague, war, strife, pillaging, and backwardness. But there was also great advancement: the creation of classical education, the beginnings of democracy and representation, the birth of universities, worldwide missions, the belief in reason, all of which together stand as the foundations of Western civilization.

As it did in the Middle Ages, the study of history serves a purpose. The Greeks, Romans, and those they inspired in *A History of Medieval Europe* saw history as a way to exemplify admirable virtues and vilify destructive traits. As you and your student(s) read, do not forget that you are not just discovering the story of Europe, but the message it teaches. The purpose of the *Teacher Manual* and *Student Guide* is to assist in that discovery.

OVERVIEW OF THE CLASS

WHAT IS HISTORY?

That may seem like a simple question to ask, but the answer, like in history, is never so simple. In lands close and abroad, men and women have argued for millennia what history is. There's a history of arguing what history is—go figure. Before you even teach history, you need to know what it is. So what is it? Is it mere facts? Is it a story? Is it moral tales? Is it the story of class struggle? Is it the story of the social lives of people groups? The first definition of history was given to us by Herodotus, a Greek historian. In the opening of *Histories*, he declared, "This is the Showing forth of the Inquiry of Herodotus of Halicarnassos, to the end that neither the deeds of men may be forgotten by lapse of time, nor the works great and marvellous, which have been produced some by Hellenes and some by Barbarians, may lose their renown; and especially that the causes may be remembered for which these waged war with one another."[1] He wrote his *Histories* to accomplish two things.

1. Remember the great (and not so great) deeds of men in order to promote better character.

2. Know the causes of events. Essentially, know our story and how we got to where we are.

For the ancients, this is what history was. To give a definition for history, *it is narrative storytelling designed to inform and inspire*. It is the biography of men, women, and people, to be learned for the practical sake of virtue formation. By studying history, we can learn what traits to emulate from the greats and what traits to avoid. Learning history is absolutely crucial to proper human development. After all, we have thousands of years of recorded human history—men and women who have faced the same trials and tumult we have, just in different form. We would be arrogant to look at the collective story that we have of humanity and then ignore it. We cherish the plays *Macbeth, Hamlet,* and *Medea* for the truths they teach us about life. Why should we not also cherish the real-life stories of Constantine, Elizabeth, and Victoria? History teaches morals and truths just as much, or even better, than our own made-up stories. We can learn from our ancestors to better our future. In short, that's history.

HOW DO I INTERPRET HISTORY?

Now that we know what history is, how do we interpret it? When approaching history and especially primary sources, you have to ask yourself eight basic questions.

1. **Who?** Who is writing it? What is his social status? What is his relation to the subject (whether it is about someone or some movement)? Is it positive or negative? Know the author.

2. **What?** What is he writing about? Know the premise.

3. **When?** Is this before, during, or after the event? What events might have shaded his interpretation? Know the time.

4. **Where?** What is the cultural context? Is he looking from the inside or the outside? Know the context.

5. **Why?** Why does he seem to be writing? Is it to convince someone? Defend someone or something? Know the purpose.

6. **Whom?** To whom is he writing? What is his intended audience? Know the target.

7. **How?** Take note of the tone. Is it sarcastic? Hyperbolic? Extremist? Know the method.

8. **Which?** Which sources does this source agree with? Disagree with? Which seem to be more trustworthy? Know the corroboration/disputation.

These eight questions may seem like a lot, but they have been formatted in such a way that a student can easily drill them off. "Who, What, When, Where, Why" is memorized in elementary school. What is absolutely fantastic about historical thinking skills is that they shape not only the mind, but also the character. Teaching students how to think like a historian teaches them how to think in general.

---

1   Herodotus, *Histories*, Book 1, Translated into English G. C. Macaulay, MacMillan and Co., London and New York, 1899.

Further, through their analysis of events and people, they learn admirable and abhorrent virtues. That is a line you can definitely use in the beginning of the class to get your students to buy in to what you are doing.

LAST TIPS
Student Preparation

Regarding student preparation, each chapter in the *Teacher Manual* will have questions marked for the test. Not all comprehension questions, key concepts, or dates will be on the test. It is up to the teacher to decide whether to inform the student of what to study. I recommend you do as the test approaches, but you can choose not to.

To promote good study habits as students read and work, I recommend the following:

- Encourage students to take notes of the reading/lecture and read those daily. Further, they should review all their written assignments in preparation. The key here is not to cram. If students attempt to cram everything a day or two ahead, it will lead to poor retention. If they diligently study every day by reading over their notes for 5-10 minutes, they will achieve better results.

- After completing all of the reading and assignments, it may help if students revise their own notes and present their own brief summary.

- To help in the memorization of key concepts, flashcards are always a worthy option.

- Overall, the most important factor that will ensure student success is diligence. If they diligently review as they go along, they will be successful.

OVERVIEW OF THE GUIDE

HOW TO USE THE STUDENT GUIDE

The *Student Guide* is broken up into several sections with instructions for each. The **Introduction** includes a **Summative Statement** exercise, a **Summative Quote** that encapsulates the chapter, and a **Hook** activity. Next, the key concepts section includes **Key Terms, Key Figures, Key Dates,** and **Key Structures**. Beyond that, there are also **Comprehension Questions, Short Answer Essay Questions,** and other activities.

Before I describe the purpose of each section, I want to first state clearly how to use the *Student Guide*.

For both the classroom and homeschool:

I have created an abundance of exercises for the student to complete. That does not mean you have to use all of them. If you wish to streamline the class or abbreviate it for ease or due to lack of time, just assign the questions in the **Questions to Mark for the Test** section and skip the rest. Alternatively or additionally, you could assign some or all of the key concepts or questions. You can choose to have students do all of the short answer essay questions or just one. The key word here is choice. You are the teacher, and you ultimately decide what is best for your students. Use, modify, and adapt the guide as needed to suit your needs.

For the classroom:

Use this book however you see fit. It probably would be best used as homework to supplement classroom instruction to ensure reading and retention. It can be used in the classroom as well.

For the homeschool:

The student is best guided through this material by discussion and conversation with a teacher, informed of the overall narrative of medieval history, in combination with the work of the *Student Guide*. The best instructor for the student is not the guide, nor the book, but you. You are the teacher. If you are unsure or lacking confidence in such a task, **Overview of the Class** is designed for you.

STUDENT GUIDE OVERVIEW

Introduction

Students will receive the **Summative Quote** of the chapter, along with a (blank) **Summative Statement**. Their first assignment after reading the chapter will be to provide a **Summative Statement**, a concise 1-2 sentences that capture the main idea.

Key Terms

For **Key Terms**, the student's job is to explain the important definitions of the chapter. The average answer should consist of 1-2 sentences unless it is a more complicated concept. Encourage students to put the definition in their own terms, trying to avoid an exact copy of what the book gives. Such effort ensures internalization and mastery of a concept.

Key Figures

Every era of history has its own colorful personalities, those "movers and shakers" who took action and provoked reactions. The student here should give a summative statement of the figure and establish his or her significance.

Key Dates

Naturally, time passes in stories. Events occur, people rise and fall, and eras come to a close. Keeping a record of important dates is necessary to ensure the story flows and holds in the student's mind. Students will be provided with each key date. It is their job to find out the significance of each one, writing a very concise sentence or phrase as they read along in the chapter. The **Key Dates** serve as the foundation for the timeline assignment, which will be explained later.

Key Structures

In every historical era, three structures of society exist: Government, Religion, and Society. The student's job will be to summarize in 1-3 sentences the dominant ideas regarding religion, government, and culture/society in each chapter. It helps students keep track of the larger changes going on in each chapter.

Comprehension Questions

These questions are designed to go along with the reading of each chapter. Generally, these straightforward questions are intended to highlight the facts. However, just because they may be straightforward does not mean the answers are to be. Do not accept 2-3 word answers. Complete sentences should be given, ranging from 3-5 sentences on average, though some questions may require a longer response. **Note:** My answers in the *Teacher Manual* are full-fledged answers. Students' answers will probably be nowhere my length. My intention was to provide as much as information as possible for the teacher.

Short Answer Essay Questions

These questions are designed to promote a higher level of interaction with the text than just a basic recounting of facts. Within 5-8 sentences, students should be able to write in their own words a micro essay, providing a succinct critical analysis of an event, era, or figure, often in relation to modern affairs.

Summative Timeline

To ensure that the students have a somewhat running timeline of Europe's history in their head, there is the summative timeline. As you will notice, in some (not every) chapter one key date is marked by asterisks. Every time students see a date marked by asterisks, they are to add it to their summative timeline. As a result, it is an ongoing assignment, only to be turned in at the end of the year. (See example in Appendix.) It should be drawn horizontally on a blank piece of paper, with a line running from left to right, having arrows at both ends. Each date should be marked on the line, with a concise statement below explaining the significance of the event. To promote retention, I would also encourage the student either drawing a picture representing the event on the top side of the timeline, or printing out and cutting out a picture from the internet. That is not necessarily required, however.

Map Activity

Our brains interpret information not only linguistically, but also visually. To guarantee that students have an accurate rendering of the socio-political map of a certain time, students will occasionally be required to fill in a map. Instructions are provided on the map activity. There is no key for this activity as you simply need to look in the textbook at the page referenced to check the student's work.

ASSESSMENTS

Assessments are conducted in two ways: quizzes and tests. The quizzes are designed to test student knowledge as they progress through the chapter(s). A quiz will be given for each chapter after its completion, which is to be taken after the reading and assignments have been completed. If the student does not do well on a quiz, that will indicate a need to review or refresh on certain concepts. Tests are intended to test student knowledge as they finish a major section. Tests will not be cumulative.

Quizzes

A quiz for each chapter will be required for students to complete. It will be derived from the reading, key concepts, and comprehension questions. Quizzes are designed to broadly test a student's knowledge after a chapter, serving as a progress analysis for the teacher. Also, these questions usually are accentuating future test questions. For the administration of quizzes, I would recommend giving one after the completion of each chapter.

Tests

The test consists of four divisions.

1. The first division entails multiple choice, though not of the typical variety. The student will be required to read through one or more primary source excerpts and choose the correct answer. The answer can be found by contextual reading and general knowledge gained from the reading of the book.

2. The second division consists of definitions, all derived from the Key Concepts section.

3. The third division contains short answer questions taken from the comprehension questions section and key concepts. Occasionally the questions will be copied verbatim from the comprehension section, usually with questions that highlight specific facts that need to be known. However, many short answer questions on tests will be an amalgam of several comprehension questions, or key concepts, requiring the students to be familiar with the overall story of an event or section of the book.

4. The fourth division involves the reproduction of the key dates (at least, what they have so far) on the summative timeline.

PART I
The Dark Ages

Baptism of Clovis at Reims (496) by Francois-Louis Dejuinne, 1837

CHAPTER 1
Constantine the Great: The New Rome and Christianity

Icon depicting the Council of Nicaea. Date and author unknown.

INTRODUCTION

Summative Statement: Provide a 1-2 sentence summary/main idea of the entire chapter.

Summative Quote

"The empire, long divided, must unite; long united, must divide. Thus it has ever been." —Luo Guanzhong, opening lines of *Romance of the Three Kingdoms*

Hook

What is more important in society: unity or truth? Explain your answer.

KEY TERMS: For each term, provide a 1-2 sentence definition.

1. Constantinople: ____

   ____

2. *Lapsi*: ____

   ____

3. *Traditor*: ____

   ____

4. *Homoousion* clause: ____

   ____

   ____

KEY FIGURES: For each figure, provide a 1-2 sentence definition; make sure to include the person's relevance and major actions in the chapter.

1. Constantine: ____

   ____

   ____

   ____

2. Arius: ____

   ____

   ____

KEY DATES: For each date, find and <u>briefly</u> explain what happened on that date.

1. 325: ____

   ____

   ____

KEY STRUCTURES: For each key structure, provide a 1-3 sentence summary of how each changed, experienced alteration, or encountered difficulty.

1. Government: ____

   ____

   ____

2. Religion: ____

   ____

   ____

   ____

3. Society: ____

   ____

   ____

COMPREHENSION QUESTIONS: Answer each question as prompted; typical answers should range from 3-8 sentences, depending on the detail of the question.

1. Why was Constantinople primarily founded?

2. Compare and contrast the cities of Constantinople and Rome.

3. What was the great purpose and function of the city of Constantinople?

4. Why were Romans, especially of the educated class, opposed to Christianity?

5. Describe the persecution the Church experienced and how the Church responded.

6. Detail what drove Constantine to convert.

7. Explain Constantine's view of his role regarding the Church.

8. Summarize the doctrinal divide within the Donatist controversy.

9. Explain the doctrinal debate of the Arian controversy.

10. What role did Constantine play in the Council of Nicaea?

____

____

____

____

____

____

____

11. Considering his overall actions toward the Church, what did Constantine seem to be concerned with? Explain.

____

____

____

____

____

____

____

____

____

SHORT ANSWER ESSAY QUESTIONS: Provide a short response in the range of 5-8 sentences.

Evaluate the authenticity of Constantine's vision.

CHAPTER 2
The Barbarian Invasions

"Destruction" from *The Course of Empire* by Thomas Cole, 1836

INTRODUCTION

Summative Statement: Provide a 1-2 sentence summary/main idea of the entire chapter.

Summative Quote

"My voice sticks in my throat; and, as I dictate, sobs choke my utterance. The City which had taken the whole world was itself taken." —St. Jerome, Letters of St. Jerome, Letter 127

Hook

Analyze the chapter picture. How does it portray the fall of Rome through its use of imagery? After reading the chapter, come back and record how well the painting matched with reality.

KEY TERMS: For each term, provide a 1-2 sentence definition.

1. *Feoderati:* ____

   ____

2. *Hospitalitas:* ____

   ____

3. *Wergeld:* ____

   ____

   ____

   ____

KEY FIGURES: For each figure, provide a 1-2 sentence definition; make sure to include the person's relevance and major actions in the chapter.

1. Aetius: ____

   ____

   ____

2. Attila the Hun: ____

   ____

3. Odovacar: ____

   ____

   ____

KEY DATES: For each date, find and <u>briefly</u> explain what happened on that date.

1. **476: ____

   ____

   ____

   ____

KEY STRUCTURES: For each key structure, provide a 1-3 sentence summary of how each changed, experienced alteration, or encountered difficulty.

1. Government:____

   ____

   ____

2. Religion: ____

   ____

   ____

3. Society: ____

   ____

   ____

COMPREHENSION QUESTIONS: Answer each question as prompted; typical answers should range from 3-8 sentences, depending on the detail of the question.

1. List the specific tribes that made up the West Germans and East Germans, and provide the main characteristic of the West Germans and East Germans.

2. What effect did the Huns have on the Germanic tribes?

3. What policies did Rome adopt as the barbarians came to its borders?

4. Reiterate the four reasons why Rome did not cease to exist overnight in 476, according to the author.

5. How did religion and law keep the Germanic peoples from fully integrating into Roman society?

SHORT ANSWER ESSAY QUESTIONS: Provide a short response in the range of 5-8 sentences.

1. Did the Romans handle the barbarian invasions/settlements the best way? Could they have done anything differently? Explain.

2. Compare and contrast the America of 1776 and the present-day America. Does the fact that it has changed make it less "American"?

____

____

____

____

____

____

____

____

____

____

____

____

____

____

____

____

____

____

____

____

____

____

SUMMATIVE TIMELINE: On a separate sheet of paper, begin a summative timeline. There will be a total of eight dates. The date to be added will be marked by two asterisks in your "Key Dates" section; alternatively, the teacher may inform you of what date is to go on the summative timeline.

MAP ACTIVITY: Using p. 29, accomplish the following:

1. Show where the Angles, Saxons, Lombards, and Burgundians originated from, and trace a line to the places they invaded.

2. Label (approximately) the Frankish kingdom, Burgundian kingdom, Ostrogothic kingdom, Visigothic kingdom, Vandal kingdom, and Persian Empire.

3. Label the following cities: Constantinople, Rome, Ravenna, Carthage, and Alexandria.

CHAPTER 3
Three Reactions to the Barbarian Invasions

Empress Theodora by Jean-Joseph Benjamin-Constant, 1887

INTRODUCTION

Summative Statement: Provide a 1-2 sentence summary/main idea of the entire chapter.

____

____

____

____

Summative Quote

"If you wish to save yourself, my lord, there is no difficulty … As for me, I agree with the adage that the royal purple is the noblest shroud." —Empress Theodora, closing lines to a speech given to Emperor Justinian and assembled advisors once they decided it would be prudent to flee from rioters who threatened to storm the Imperial Palace. After her words, Justinian composed himself and ordered the troops to slaughter the rebels.

Hook

Compare and contrast the paintings. Do you see more paintings akin to the left or right one based on your experience? Note: The one on the left is from Western Europe, while the one on the right is from Eastern Europe.

Left: *The Crucifixion* by Bartolomé Esteban Murillo, c. 1675

Right: Chora Church/Kariye Camii, Istanbul, Turkey

KEY TERMS: For each term, provide a 1-2 sentence definition.

1. *Vivarium:* ____

    ____

    ____

2. Hagia Sophia: ____

    ____

    ____

KEY FIGURES: For each figure, provide a 1-2 sentence definition; make sure to include the person's relevance and major actions in the chapter.

1. St. Augustine: ____

    ____

    ____

2. Theodoric: ____

    ____

    ____

3. Cassiodorus: ____

    ____

    ____

4. Justinian: ____

____

____

5. Theodora: ____

____

____

____

KEY DATES: For each date, find and <u>briefly</u> explain what happened on that date.

1. **525: ____

____

KEY STRUCTURES: For each key structure, provide a 1-3 sentence summary of how each changed, experienced alteration, or encountered difficulty.

1. Government:____

____

2. Religion: ____

____

____

3. Society: ____

____

____

____

COMPREHENSION QUESTIONS: Answer each question as prompted; typical answers should range from 3-8 sentences, depending on the detail of the question.

1. In what historical context was _City of God_ written? What prompted its writing?

2. Outline the main arguments and conclusion of *City of God.*

3. Why was Theodoric popular in Italy?

4. What were two underlying problems for Theodoric's rule?

5. Why did Theodoric come to fear the Church? What was Theodoric's last act?

6. What did Cassiodorus seek to accomplish by founding his monastery?

____

____

____

____

____

7. Summarize the reconquest of North Africa and Italy during the reign of Justinian.

____

____

____

____

____

____

____

8. Explain what the _Corpus Juris Civilis_ was and its three major sections.

____

____

____

____

____

____

9. What was the long-term effect of Justinian's law code?

____

____

____

10. What made Justinian's latter reign unsuccessful?

____

____

____

____

____

____

____

____

____

____

SHORT ANSWER ESSAY QUESTIONS: Provide a short response in the range of 5-8 sentences.

In your view, which of the three responses to the barbarian invasions was the best? The worst? Why?

SUMMATIVE TIMELINE: Continue your summative timeline.

CHAPTER 4
The Church and the Papacy

The Temptation of St. Anthony by Matthias Grünewald, 1515

INTRODUCTION

Summative Statement: Provide a 1-2 sentence summary/main idea of the entire chapter.

Summative Quote

"He should know that whoever undertakes the government of souls must prepare himself to account for them."
—St. Benedict of Nursia

Hook

Examine the painting above. What is the intended meaning of the symbolism the artist employs to depict the temptation of St. Anthony?

KEY TERMS: For each term, provide a 1-2 sentence definition.

1. Metropolitan: ____

   ____

2. Cenobitic: ____

3. *Pallium*: ____

   ____

   ____

KEY FIGURES: For each figure, provide a 1-2 sentence definition; make sure to include the person's relevance and major actions in the chapter.

1. St. Benedict: ____

   ____

   ____

2. Gregory the Great:____

   ____

   ____

KEY DATES: For each date, find and <u>briefly</u> explain what happened on that date.

1. 590-604: ____

   ____

KEY STRUCTURES: For each key structure, provide a 1-3 sentence summary of how each changed, experienced alteration, or encountered difficulty.

1. Government:____

   ____

   ____

   ____

2. Religion: ____

   ____

   ____

   ____

   ____

3. Society: ____

   ____

   ____

COMPREHENSION QUESTIONS: Answer each question as prompted; typical answers should range from 3-8 sentences, depending on the detail of the question.

1. Describe the life and function of a typical church during the second century.

2. Why did bishops become so significant in the early church? Why did the idea of apostolic succession come about?

3. Explain the reasons why some bishops became more important than others.

4. What was the Church of Rome's argument for papal primacy?

5. What advantage did Rome have being in the West?

6. Who was St. Benedict influenced by when creating his monastic system? What made his different?

7. Outline the steps St. Benedict created in his Rule to encourage humility among the monks.

8. What was the main achievement of Benedictine monasticism?

9. What was the condition of Rome during the life of Gregory the Great?

10. Describe the life of Gregory the Great until he became pope.

11. Why did Gregory assume the responsibilities of the imperial government?

12. Outline the Church government that came about under Gregory the Great.

13. How did missionaries from England contribute to the development of the medieval Church, with its centralized leadership found in the pope?

Discuss what St. Benedict and Gregory the Great emphasized as they made changes within the Church.

CHAPTER 5
Islam

Maryam and Isa, old Persian miniature. Date unknown.

Summative Quote

She conceived him, and retired with him to a far-off place.

And the throes came upon her by the trunk of a palm.

She said: "Oh, would that I had died ere this, and been a thing forgotten, forgotten quite!"

And one cried to her from below her:

"Grieve not thou, thy Lord hath provided a streamlet at thy feet: And shake the trunk of the palm-tree toward thee: it will drop fresh ripe dates upon thee.

Eat then and drink, and be of cheerful eye: and shouldst thou see a man,

Say, 'Verily, I have vowed abstinence to the God of mercy. To no one will I speak this day.'"

Then came she with the babe to her people, bearing him. They said, "O Mary! now hast thou done a strange thing! O sister of Aaron! Thy father was not a man of wickedness, nor unchaste thy mother."

And she made a sign to them, pointing towards the babe. They said, "How shall we speak with him who is in the cradle, an infant?"

It said, "Verily, I am the servant of God; He hath given me the Book, and He hath made me a prophet; And He hath made me blessed wherever I may be, and hath enjoined me prayer and almsgiving so long as I shall live; And to be duteous to her that bare me: and he hath not made me proud, depraved. And the peace of God was on me the day I was born, and will be the day I shall die, and the day I shall be raised to life."

This is Jesus, the son of Mary; this is a statement of the truth concerning which they doubt. It beseemeth not God to beget a son. Glory be to Him! when he decreeth a thing, He only saith to it, Be, and it Is.

—Koran, *Sura Mary*, 19:22-33

INTRODUCTION

Summative Statement: Provide a 1-2 sentence summary/main idea of the entire chapter.

Hook

Contrast the Koran's account of Jesus' birth with the biblical account.

KEY TERMS: For each term, provide a 1-2 sentence definition.

1. Islam: ____

   ____

2. *Kaaba*: ____

   ____

3. *Hejira*:____

   ____

   ____

4. Caliph: ____

   ____

5. *Imam*: ____

   ____

6. Shi'as:____

   ____

7. *Mawali*:____

   ____

KEY FIGURES: For each figure, provide a 1-2 sentence definition; make sure to include the person's relevance and major actions in the chapter.

1. Mohammed: ____

   ____

2. Heraclius: ____

   ____

   ____

KEY DATES: For each date, find and <u>briefly</u> explain what happened on that date.

1. **570: ____

   ____

KEY STRUCTURES: For each key structure, provide a 1-3 sentence summary of how each changed, experienced alteration, or encountered difficulty.

1. Government:____

   ____

   ____

2. Religion: ____

   ____

   ____

   ____

3. Society: ____

____

____

____

____

COMPREHENSION QUESTIONS: Answer each question as prompted; typical answers should range from 3-8 sentences, depending on the detail of the question.

1. Summarize Mohammed's life before the age of forty.

2. Outline the life of Mohammed from 610-622, including the *Hejira*.

3. Briefly describe the events of Mohammed's life from 622-632.

4. Which Islamic beliefs were heavily influenced by the Arabic cultural context?

5. What were other common Islamic beliefs?

6. Explain the importance of the Koran, its structure, and how its views changed toward Christians and Jews.

7. Briefly highlight the Islamic view of church and state.

8. What lands had Islam acquired by the 640s? By 720?

9. Delineate the reasons for Islam's amazing conquests.

10. Summarize the Islamic Empire from 632-661.

11. What did the Omayyad caliphs emphasize during their reign?

____

____

____

____

____

____

12. Highlight the characteristics that marked the Abbasid caliphate.

____

____

____

____

____

____

____

____

13. Describe the overall socio-cultural effects of the Islamic conquests upon the Arabs and their conquered subjects.

____

____

____

____

____

SHORT ANSWER ESSAY QUESTIONS: Provide a short response in the range of 5-8 sentences.
Based on this chapter, compare and contrast the beliefs of Christianity and Islam.

____

____

____

____

____

____

____

____

____

____

____

____

____

____

____

____

____

____

____

____

SUMMATIVE TIMELINE: Continue your summative timeline.

MAP ACTIVITY: Using pp. 104-105, accomplish the following:

1. Shade in the holdings of: the Byzantine Empire, the former Persian Empire, the Franks, and all the lands conquered by Islam. Distinguish between Islam and the former Persian Empire.

2. Label the following locations or groups: the Byzantine Empire, former Persian Empire, Islamic Empire, Franks, Lombards, Bulgars, Visigoths, battle of Poitiers, Cordova, and Baghdad.

CHAPTER 6
The Franks

Emperor Charlemagne by Albrecht Dürer, 1511/1513

INTRODUCTION

Summative Statement: Provide a 1-2 sentence summary/main idea of the entire chapter.

Summative Quote

"Under a pine-tree, near an eglantine,
Is placed a faldstool of pure gold whereon
Sits he, the King—great Ruler of Sweet France.
White is his beard, his head all flowering white;

Graceful his form and proud his countenance;
None need to point him out to those who come..."
—from *The Song of Roland*, Stanza 8

Hook

Analyze/break down the chapter picture. Make sure to pay close attention to the symbolism.

KEY TERMS: For each term, provide a 1-2 sentence definition.

1. Merovingians: ____

   ____

   ____

2. First Saxon capitulary: ____

   ____

   ____

KEY FIGURES: For each figure, provide a 1-2 sentence definition; make sure to include the person's relevance and major actions in the chapter.

1. Clovis: ____

   ____

   ____

2. Alcuin: ____

   ____

   ____

3. Pope Leo III: ____

   ____

   ____

KEY DATES: For each date, find and <u>briefly</u> explain what happened on that date.

1. **800: ____

   ____

   ____

KEY STRUCTURES: For each key structure, provide a 1-3 sentence summary of how each changed, experienced alteration, or encountered difficulty.

1. Government: ____

   ____

   ____

   ____

   ____

   ____

2. Religion: ____

   ____

   ____

   ____

3. Society: ____

____

____

____

COMPREHENSION QUESTIONS: Answer each question as prompted; typical answers should range from 3-8 sentences, depending on the detail of the question.

1. What caused the Merovingian dynasty to suffer from so many civil wars?

____

____

2. Describe the relationship between the Franks and the Gallo-Roman population; further, describe how the Frankish kings viewed the land of Gaul/France.

____

____

____

____

____

____

3. Outline the political administration of the Frankish Kingdom.

____

____

____

____

____

____

____

____

4. What role(s) did bishops play in Frankish society?

____

____

____

____

____

____

____

5. Why did the bishops support the Frankish state?

6. What did nobles begin to demand of the Merovingian kings by the 600s-700s?

7. Explain the cause(s) and development of the vassalage system.

8. Describe the equipment and training/tactics of a knight.

9. How does the author explain feudalism and its origin?

10. How did the Carolingians view themselves?

11. Detail the process of Pepin III's coronation as the first Carolingian king.

12. How did Charlemagne view himself and his purpose in life?

13. In what ways did Charlemagne seek to revive learning during his reign?

14. What series of events led to Charlemagne's presence in Rome in 800?

15. Explain the two main views of Charlemagne's coronation.

16. What was the ultimate significance of Charlemagne's coronation?

SHORT ANSWER ESSAY QUESTIONS: Provide a short response in the range of 5-8 sentences.

1. In this chapter, explain why Charlemagne seemed to believe church and state should be united.

2. Do you agree or disagree with Charlemagne's conclusion that he was a new David over a new Israel?

SUMMATIVE TIMELINE: Continue your summative timeline.

MAP ACTIVITY: Using p. 150, accomplish the following:

1. Shade in the holdings of: the Kingdom of the Franks and the acquisitions of Charlemagne.
2. Label the following locations: Aachen, Tours, Poitiers, Toulouse, Paris, Milan, and Rome.

CHAPTER 7
The Break-Up of the Carolingian Empire

Thor's Fight with the Giants by Marten Eskil Winge, 1872

INTRODUCTION

Summative Statement: Provide a 1-2 sentence summary/main idea of the entire chapter.

Summative Quote

"Hard is it in the world, great whoredom, an axe age, a sword age, shields shall be cloven, a wind age, a wolf age, ere the world sinks." —The Poetic Edda

Hook

Analyze/break down the chapter picture. Then explain how the quote above relates to the chapter picture.

KEY TERMS: For each term, provide a 1-2 sentence definition.

1. Partition of Verdun: ____

   ____

   ____

2. Normandy: ____

   ____

3. *Danegeld:* ____

   ____

4. *Burhs:* ____

   ____

KEY FIGURES: For each figure, provide a 1-2 sentence definition; make sure to include the person's relevance and major actions in the chapter.

1. Louis the Pious: ____

   ____

   ____

   ____

2. Alfred the Great: ____

   ____

KEY DATES: For each date, find and <u>briefly</u> explain what happened on that date.

1. **843: ____

   ____

   ____

KEY STRUCTURES: For each key structure, provide a 1-3 sentence summary of how each changed, experienced alteration, or encountered difficulty.

1. Government: ____

   ____

   ____

   ____

2. Religion: ____

   ____

   ____

3. Society: ____

   ____

   ____

   ____

COMPREHENSION QUESTIONS: Answer each question as prompted; typical answers should range from 3-8 sentences, depending on the detail of the question.

1. What were some of Louis' reforms? How did his belief in Christ influence his governmental and legal policy?

2. What was Louis' greatest concern? What did he attempt to do?

3. Briefly describe the fate of Louis' empire. Further, detail how it was divided.

4. Why did the vassals of the Frankish kingdom swear loyalty to the Carolingian kings, whether it was Charles the Bald or Louis the German?

5. What were the three invasions, and from what direction did they come?

____

____

6. Summarize the general areas the Vikings attacked and invaded.

____

____

____

____

____

____

____

____

____

7. Summarize the general areas the Saracens (Muslims) attacked and invaded.

____

____

____

____

8. Summarize the general areas the Hungarians attacked and invaded.

____

____

____

9. Why were the Carolingian kingdoms unable to establish a strong defense? To specify, what enabled the Vikings to be so successful at raiding?

____

____

____

____

____

____

10. What system of defense was widely employed by the kings of Europe? What did they require to function properly?

____

____

____

____

____

____

11. Why did the concept of a universal monarchy and kingdom come to an end in this age?

____

____

____

____

____

____

____

SHORT ANSWER ESSAY QUESTIONS: Provide a short response in the range of 5-8 sentences.

Speculate on other reasons why the Vikings raided and explored so much.

____

____

____

____

____

____

____

____

____

____

____

____

____

____

____

____

____

____

____

____

____

____

____

____

SUMMATIVE TIMELINE: Continue your summative timeline.

MAP ACTIVITY: Using pp. 176-177, accomplish the following:

1. Trace the invasion routes of: the Vikings, Hungarians, and Saracens (Muslims).
2. Label the following locations: Aachen, Rouen, Paris, London, York, Rome, and Constantinople.

CHAPTER 8
Europe at the End of the Ninth Century: Economic Survey

Harun al-Rashid Receiving a Delegation of Charlemagne in Baghdad by Julius Kockert, 1864

INTRODUCTION

Summative Statement: Provide a 1-2 sentence summary/main idea of the entire chapter.

Summative Quote

"Some years before he (Harun al-Rashid) had sent, besides other rich and costly presents, one which especially impressed the minds of the Franks, an enormous elephant named Abu-l-Abbas (to Charlemagne). Under the guidance of its keeper, Isaac the Jew, the elephant safely reached Aachen, where it abode for eight years. In the year 810 it was taken across the Rhine, apparently that its great strength might be made use of in the expected campaign against Godofrid the Dane; and its sudden death at Lippeham in Westphalia is solemnly recorded by the chroniclers among the memorable events of that melancholy year." —Thomas Hodgkin, *The Life of Charlemagne*, 1902

Hook

What was the purpose of Harun al-Rashid sending Charlemagne an elephant? What truth does this reveal about trade between Western Europe and the Middle East in the "Dark Ages"?

KEY TERMS: For each term, provide a 1-2 sentence definition.

1. Demesne land: ____

   ____

2. Tributary land: ____

   ____

3. *Mansus*: ____

   ____

   ____

COMPREHENSION QUESTIONS: Answer each question as prompted; typical answers should range from 3-8 sentences, depending on the detail of the question.

1. Describe the state of the Byzantine economy; make sure to note the involvement of the government as well.

2. Describe the state of the Islamic Empire's economy.

3. Explain Pirenne's theory on the poverty of the Latin West's economy.

4. Highlight at least three objections to Pirenne's theory.

5. Why was the use of money quite limited in the Latin West?

6. Summarize the relationship between lord and tenant on tributary lands.

7. Expound upon how ninth-century agrarian society was in a state of transition.

8. Describe the open-field system.

9. Explain the enclosure system.

PART II
The High Middle Ages

The Return of the Crusader by Karl Friedrich Lessing, 1835

CHAPTER 1
The Saxon Empire

Opening of the Tomb of Charlemagne by Otto III by Alfred Rethel, 1870

INTRODUCTION

Summative Statement: Provide a 1-2 sentence summary/main idea of the entire chapter.

Summative Quote

We saw Charlemagne "... seated in a certain chair as though he lived. He was crowned with a golden crown, and held a sceptre in his hands, the same being covered with gloves, through which the nails had grown and pierced. ... So we did worship to him with bended thighs and knees; and straightway Otto the Emperor clad him with white raiment, and pared his nails, and made good all that was lacking about him." —Chronicon Novaliciense, from *A History of Medieval Europe*, pp. 252-253

Hook

Read the Introduction to Part Two, pp. 225-232. What is the difference between the goal of the Capetian policy of kingship and the German policy of kingship? Further, consider the quote above. How did Charlemagne affect the German view?

KEY TERMS: For each term, provide a 1-2 sentence definition.

1. Hungarians: ____

    ____

    ____

2. Ottonian government: ____

    ____

    ____

3. *Ottonianum*: ____

    ____

    ____

    ____

KEY FIGURES: For each figure, provide a 1-2 sentence definition; make sure to include the person's relevance and major actions in the chapter.

1. Otto the Great: ____

    ____

    ____

2. Pope John XII: ____

    ____

    ____

3. Theophano: ____

    ____

    ____

KEY DATES: For each date, find and <u>briefly</u> explain what happened on that date.

1. 962: ____

KEY STRUCTURES: For each key structure, provide a 1-3 sentence summary of how each changed, experienced alteration, or encountered difficulty.

1. Government: ____

    ____

    ____

2. Religion: ____

    ____

    ____

3. Society: ____

    ____

    ____

COMPREHENSION QUESTIONS: Answer each question as prompted; typical answers should range from 3-8 sentences, depending on the detail of the question.

1. What were the five duchies of the Holy Roman Empire? What was the difference between the first four and the fifth one?

2. Explain the royal rights Henry the Fowler had over his dukes.

3. Outline the election ceremony of Otto the Great, paying particular attention to where he received his power from.

4. How did Otto the Great handle rebellious nobles before the rebellion of his son, Liudolf?

5. Summarize the events beginning in 950, consisting of the revolt of Otto's son, Liudolf.

____

____

____

____

____

____

____

____

____

____

____

6. What was the experiment Otto conducted in Lotharingia? How did he see this as advantageous?

____

____

____

____

____

____

____

____

7. How did immunity affect the governing of the bishops? What were the bishops' and abbots' powers?

____

____

____

____

____

____

8. Explain how the bishops' powers were limited and what they owed to the king.

____

____

____

____

9. What problems arose concerning the bishopric government? To whom did Otto turn for assistance?

____

____

____

____

____

____

____

____

10. Outline the tumultuous relationship between Otto the Great and the papacy.

____

____

____

____

____

____

____

____

____

____

____

____

11. In the eyes of the Ottos, particularly Otto III, what was the mission of him, his family, and the Holy
    Roman Empire?

____

____

____

____

____

____

SHORT ANSWER ESSAY QUESTIONS: Provide a short response in the range of 5-8 sentences.

Europe under Charlemagne became a historical ideal to aspire to or emulate. Identify another time in history that is idealized by people today. How can pursuing that ideal affect society?

CHAPTER 2
The Reform of the Papacy

Henry at Canossa by Eduard Schwoiser, 1862

INTRODUCTION

Summative Statement: Provide a 1-2 sentence summary/main idea of the entire chapter.

Summative Quote

"I have loved justice and hated iniquity, and therefore I die in exile." —Last words of Pope Gregory VII, 1085

Hook

Analyze the quote of Pope Gregory VII. What greater truth is he speaking to?

KEY TERMS: For each term, provide a 1-2 sentence definition.

1. Simony: ____

   ____

2. Lay investiture: ____

3. Canon Law:____

   ____

   ____

KEY FIGURES: For each figure, provide a 1-2 sentence definition; make sure to include the person's relevance and major actions in the chapter.

1. Pope Leo IX: ____

   ____

   ____

   ____

2. Pope Gregory VII: _______________________________________

   ____

   ____

3. Henry IV: ____

   ____

   ____

KEY STRUCTURES: For each key structure, provide a 1-3 sentence summary of how each changed, experienced alteration, or encountered difficulty.

1. Government:____

   ____

   ____

   ____

2. Religion: ____

   ____

   ____

   ____

3. Society: ____

   ____

   ____

COMPREHENSION QUESTIONS: Answer each question as prompted; typical answers should range from 3-8 sentences, depending on the detail of the question.

1. How were popes elected before Pope Nicholas II?

2. Explain the official declaration of the election decree of 1059 as well as the expressed and unexpressed intent.

3. How did the imperials view the election decree of 1059? How did Nicholas II handle the imperial response?

4. What did Nicholas II's pontificate mark the beginning of?

5. What two major problems did Gregory VII and others seek to reform in the Church? How did they contribute to corruption in the Church as well?

6. What doctrine did the reformers believe was the long-term solution to lay investiture? How did they seek to support it?

7. How did Gregory VII use Canon Law to strengthen the papacy? What occurred at the Lenten Council of 1075?

8. When the Investiture Controversy broke out, what was the claim of the imperialists? Of the reformers?

9. Who took advantage of Pope Gregory VII's deposition of Henry IV? What were their actions?

10. Why did Henry IV seek out Gregory VII?

11. Summarize the response of Gregory VII to Henry IV's penitence.

12. How did Henry IV come to be excommunicated a second time?

13. What was the significance of Pope Urban II's election and papacy?

14. How did Henry IV's rebellion against the pope change the persona of the emperor?

What are some of the possible consequences (positive or negative) of a church-state union, in light of the chapter?

CHAPTER 3
Monasticism in the Eleventh and Twelfth Centuries

Bernard of Clairvaux Converts William of Aquitaine by Wouter Crabeth II, 1641

INTRODUCTION

Summative Statement: Provide a 1-2 sentence summary/main idea of the entire chapter.

Summative Quote

"Listen, my son, to your master's precepts, and incline the ear of your heart. Receive willingly and carry out effectively your loving father's advice, that by the labor of obedience you may return to Him from whom you had departed by the sloth of disobedience. To you, therefore, my words are now addressed, whoever you may be, who are renouncing your own will to do battle under the Lord Christ, the true King, and are taking up the strong, bright weapons of obedience."
—Rule of St. Benedict, St. Benedict, 516

Hook

Read the summative quote. What will enable the reader to "... return to Him?" How is this life described through the language?

KEY TERMS: For each term, provide a 1-2 sentence definition.

1. Cluny: ____

    ____

    ____

2. *Carta Caritatis:*_______________________________________

    ____

    ____

    ____

KEY FIGURES: For each figure, provide a 1-2 sentence definition; make sure to include the person's relevance and major actions in the chapter.

1. St. Berno: _______________________________________

    ____

    ____

2. St. Bernard of Clairvaux: _______________________________

    ____

    ____

    ____

KEY STRUCTURES: For each key structure, provide a 1-3 sentence summary of how each changed, experienced alteration, or encountered difficulty.

1. Government:_____________________________________

    ____

    ____

2. Religion: _______________________________________

    ____

    ____

3. Society: _______________________________________

    ____

    ____

COMPREHENSION QUESTIONS: Answer each question as prompted; typical answers should range from 3-8 sentences, depending on the detail of the question.

1. How did St. Bernard view the monastic life?

2. How did medieval lords and people view monks?

3. What was new about monasticism in the tenth, eleventh, and twelfth centuries?

4. How did the Cluniacs reform other monasteries?

5. Describe the formation and structure of Cluniac government.

6. What distinguished the Cistercians from the Cluniacs in their day-to-day lives?

7. How did the desire to be like St. Benedict and the early Church affect the actions of the Cistercian Order?

8. How did the architecture and interior design of the Cistercians differ from the Cluniacs?

9. Describe the relationship of the Abbot of Citeaux with the other abbots and monasteries.

10. Explain how the Cistercian Order founded other monasteries.

SHORT ANSWER ESSAY QUESTIONS: Provide a short response in the range of 5-8 sentences.

Compare and contrast a miracle from the New Testament with "A Miracle of St. Bernard" in the chapter's Appendix. Who caused each miracle? Can you discern a clear purpose with each miracle?

CHAPTER 4
Jerusalem Regained and Lost: The First Three Crusades

Taking of Jerusalem by the Crusaders (July 15, 1099) by Emile Signol, 1847

INTRODUCTION

Summative Statement: Provide a 1-2 sentence summary/main idea of the entire chapter.

Summative Quote

"Very soon, when the Saracens saw the Franks breaching the walls, they quickly fled over the walls and through the city. While they were retreating, our entire army rushed in, some through the breaches made by the battering rams, others by jumping from the tops of their machines ... The Franks chased the fleeing pagans fiercely, killing everyone they came upon, more in slaughter than in battle, through the streets, squares, and crossroads, until they reached what was called the Temple of Solomon. So much human blood flowed that a wave of damp gore almost covered the ankles of the advancing men. That was the nature of their success that day ... They approached the sepulchre of the Lord and thanked Him for what they had sought, the liberation of the Blessed Places; He had performed such great deeds with them as his instruments, that neither those who had performed them nor any other men could properly evaluate these great deeds." —The Deeds of God Through the Franks, Guibert of Nogent, 1107-1108

Hook

Read the summative quote. How can the author consider the crusaders' actions at the siege of Jerusalem "great deeds" and at the same time a "slaughter"? After reading the chapter, return to the quote and explain whether your view of the crusaders changed.

KEY TERMS: For each term, provide a 1-2 sentence definition.

1. Old-stagers: ____

   ____

   ____

2. *Jihad*: ____

   ____

KEY FIGURES: For each figure, provide a 1-2 sentence definition; make sure to include the person's relevance and major actions in the chapter.

1. Bishop Adhemar Le Puy: ____

   ____

2. Emperor Alexius: ____

   ____

3. Saladin: ____

   ____

   ____

KEY DATES: For each date, find and <u>briefly</u> explain what happened on that date.

1. **1095: ____

   ____

KEY STRUCTURES: For each key structure, provide a 1-3 sentence summary of how each changed, experienced alteration, or encountered difficulty.

1. Government: ____

   ____

2. Religion: ____

   ____

   ____

3. Society: ____

   ____

   ____

   ____

   ____

COMPREHENSION QUESTIONS: Answer each question as prompted; typical answers should range from 3-8 sentences, depending on the detail of the question.

1. Why hadn't a Crusade been called before 1095? Why was the First Crusade called in 1095?

2. What did Pope Urban II preach, promise, and call for?

3. Outline all the crusading armies and leaders of the First Crusade.

4. Why did Alexius respond in such a negative way to the crusaders' arrival?

5. How did Alexius seek to ensure loyalty from the crusaders? What did that agreement stipulate?

6. How did the Latins and Greeks view each other?

7. How did inter-Muslim relations affect the outcome of the First Crusade?

8. Explain the division of the Holy Land among the leaders.

9. Outline how King Baldwin I stabilized and defended the Kingdom of Jerusalem.

10. Detail old-stager crusader/Muslim relations within the crusader kingdoms.

____

____

____

____

____

11. How did the views of new crusaders differ from the old-stagers?

____

____

____

____

____

____

12. How did the division between the old-stagers and new crusaders affect the outcome of the Second Crusade?

____

____

____

____

____

____

____

____

13. What was the true threat for the crusaders during the 1100s? Who enabled this new threat, becoming its leader?

____

____

____

____

14. With the rise of Saladin, what policy was advocated? Why?

____

____

____

____

____

15. How did Count Raymond of Tripoli contribute to the fall of Jerusalem?

16. Why did the Third Crusade fail?

17. How had the Crusades come to be viewed by the end of the Third Crusade?

SHORT ANSWER ESSAY QUESTIONS: Provide a short response in the range of 5-8 sentences.

Recount the battle of Antioch, and evaluate the claim of the crusaders that St. George and saints had come to their aid.

SUMMATIVE TIMELINE: Continue your summative timeline.

MAP ACTIVITY: Using p. 305 and p. 311, accomplish the following:

1. On the first map, trace the route of the First Crusade and label the following locations: Paris, Rome, Constantinople, Nicaea, Antioch, Acre, Damascus, and Jerusalem.

2. On the second map, label the following locations: Kingdom of Jerusalem, County of Tripoli, Principality of Antioch, and County of Edessa.

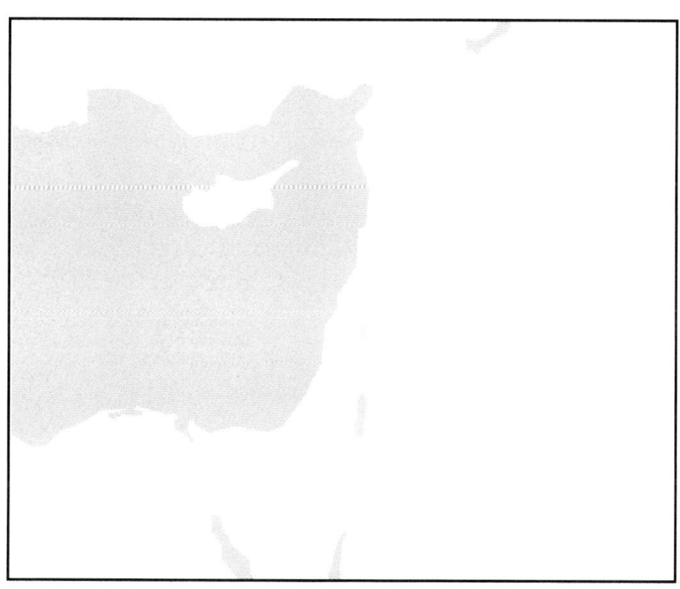

CHAPTER 5
Feudal Monarchy and the French Kingdom (1066-1223)

Battle of Bouvines by Horace Vernet, 1827

INTRODUCTION

Summative Statement: Provide a 1-2 sentence summary/main idea of the entire chapter.

Summative Quote

"The church of Notre-Dame de Paris is still no doubt, a majestic and sublime edifice. But, beautiful as it has been preserved in growing old, it is difficult not to sigh, not to wax indignant, before the numberless degradations and mutilations which time and men have both caused the venerable monument to suffer, without respect for Charlemagne, who laid its first stone, or for Philip Augustus, who laid the last. On the face of this aged queen of our cathedrals, by the side of a wrinkle, one always finds a scar. Tempus edax, homo edacior; which I should be glad to translate thus: time is blind, man is stupid." —Victor Hugo, *The Hunchback of Notre-Dame*, 1831

Hook

Read the summative quote, and explain what truth about life Victor Hugo sought to communicate.

KEY TERMS: For each term, provide a 1-2 sentence definition.

1. Domesday Book: ____

    ____

    ____

2. The Capetians: ____

    ____

    ____

KEY FIGURES: For each figure, provide a 1-2 sentence definition; make sure to include the person's relevance and major actions in the chapter.

1. William the Conqueror: ____

    ____

    ____

2. Eleanor of Aquitaine: ____

    ____

    ____

    ____

    ____

3. Philip II Augustus: ____

    ____

    ____

KEY DATES: For each date, find and <u>briefly</u> explain what happened on that date.

1. **1180-1223: ____

    ____

KEY STRUCTURES: For each key structure, provide a 1-3 sentence summary of how each changed, experienced alteration, or encountered difficulty.

1. Government:____

    ____

    ____

2. Religion: ____

    ____

    ____

3. Society: ____

    ____

    ____

    ____

COMPREHENSION QUESTIONS: Answer each question as prompted; typical answers should range from 3-8 sentences, depending on the detail of the question.

1. How did William the Conqueror form the best and simplest example of feudal monarchy?

2. Provide examples of how much control William had over his tenants and their land.

3. Outline the power and relations of the Capetian dynasty, its vassals/nobles, and the Church at the onset of the Capetian reign.

4. How did the Capetians, particularly Louis VI, seek to master their demesne?

5. Explain the effects of the loss of Eleanor of Aquitaine to Henry II of England.

6. What discouraged French lords from swearing fealty to Henry II of England?

7. What general tactic did Philip II Augustus adopt to weaken the English?

8. Summarize how Philip II used feudalism to justifiably declare war on King John of England.

9. Why did Philip II utilize such a drawn-out strategy to simply declare war on King John?

10. What territory became the main target of Philip II? Why?

11. Detail the effects of Philip II's victory at the battle of Bouvines.

12. Explain the cultural flourishing that occurred during the reign of Philip II Augustus.

13. How did Philip II ensure that his kingdom prospered long term?

SHORT ANSWER ESSAY QUESTIONS: Provide a short response in the range of 5-8 sentences.

Read "A Charter of Philip Augustus" in the chapter's Appendix. In what or whom did Philip II root his authority for the publication and enforcement of the charter? Why? How did that reinforce the legitimacy of the charter?

____

____

____

____

____

____

____

____

____

____

SUMMATIVE TIMELINE: Continue your summative timeline.

MAP ACTIVITY: Using p. 332, accomplish the following:

1. Outline the dominions of King Henry II of England, the royal demesne, and the frontier of the French Kingdom.

2. Label the following locations: Paris, Orleans, London, Citeaux, Cluny, Toulouse, and Lyons.

CHAPTER 6
The Emperor Frederick I Barbarossa (1152-1190)

Emperor Frederick I, Known as "Barbarossa" by Christian Siedentopf, 1847

INTRODUCTION

Summative Statement: Provide a 1-2 sentence summary/main idea of the entire chapter.

Summative Quote

"This body which called itself and which still calls itself the Holy Roman Empire was in no way holy, nor Roman, nor an empire." —Voltaire (1694-1778)

Hook

Do you agree or disagree with the claim of Voltaire? Explain why or why not.

KEY TERMS: For each term, provide a 1-2 sentence definition.

1. Austria: ____

    ____

    ____

2. *Privilegium Minus*: ____

    ____

    ____

    ____

    ____

3. Lombard League: ____

    ____

    ____

KEY FIGURES: For each figure, provide a 1-2 sentence definition; make sure to include the person's relevance and major actions in the chapter.

1. Frederick I Barbarossa: ____

    ____

    ____

2. Henry the Lion: ____

    ____

    ____

KEY DATES: For each date, find and <u>briefly</u> explain what happened on that date.

1. 1152-1190: ____

    ____

KEY STRUCTURES: For each key structure, provide a 1-3 sentence summary of how each changed, experienced alteration, or encountered difficulty.

1. Government:____

    ____

    ____

2. Religion: ____

    ____

    ____

3. Society: ____

    ____

    ____

    ____

COMPREHENSION QUESTIONS: Answer each question as prompted; typical answers should range from 3-8 sentences, depending on the detail of the question.

1. Define the Guelfs and Ghibellines and who they supported respectively.

2. What was the state of the Holy Roman Empire upon the election of Frederick Barbarossa?

3. How did Frederick Barbarossa attempt to manage the Guelf-Hohenstaufen divide?

4. Briefly summarize what was done to appease Henry Jasomirgott.

5. Why was Frederick so generous with the nobles regarding his lost rights? What did he hope to gain?

6. How had the nobles expanded their power base?

7. What specific policy did Frederick adopt regarding Henry the Lion early in his reign?

8. What policy did Frederick adopt in Italy? What belief motivated the adoption of the policy?

9. How did Roman Law affect the views and actions of Frederick Barbarossa?

10. Explain the political government and ideology of the northern Italian republics/communes.

11. How did Frederick end up losing his authority in Italy and to the papacy?

12. Summarize how Frederick ended the conflict in Italy.

13. Delineate upon how Frederick removed Henry the Lion from power.

14. What was the first factor that enabled Frederick to declare such a harsh sentence toward Henry the Lion?

15. What was the second factor that enabled Frederick to declare such a harsh sentence toward Henry the Lion?

16. How did this affect the Holy Roman Empire long term?

____

____

____

____

____

17. How did the princes of the Holy Roman Empire act toward the Hohenstaufens after the death of Henry VI? Why?

____

____

____

____

____

____

____

____

____

____

SHORT ANSWER ESSAY QUESTIONS: Provide a short response in the range of 5-8 sentences.

Compare and contrast the reign of Philip II Augustus and Frederick I Barbarossa.

____

____

____

____

____

____

____

____

____

____

____

____

____

____

____

____

____

CHAPTER 7
The Crisis of the Church

Saint Francis of Assisi in Ecstasy by Caravaggio, 1594

INTRODUCTION

Summative Statement: Provide a 1-2 sentence summary/main idea of the entire chapter.

Summative Quote

"They assert and confess that there are two Gods or two Lords, viz. a good God, and an evil Creator of all things visible and material; declaring that these things (the physical world) were not made by God our heavenly Father ... but by a wicked devil, even Satan ... and so they assume two Creators, viz. God and the Devil; and two Creations, viz. one of immaterial and invisible things, the other of visible and material."* —From *The Albigensian Heresy*, Henry James Warner, 1922

*Abbreviation for videlicet, which means "that is to say" or "namely"

Hook

What are the implications for the Christian faith if God the Father did not create the physical world, but Satan?

1. Manichaeism: ____

   ____

   ____

2. *Waldenses*: ____

   ____

   ____

KEY FIGURES: For each figure, provide a 1-2 sentence definition; make sure to include the person's relevance and major actions in the chapter.

1. Innocent III: ____

   ____

   ____

2. St. Francis: ____

   ____

   ____

   ____

3. Ugolino: ____

   ____

   ____

   ____

KEY DATES: For each date, find and <u>briefly</u> explain what happened on that date.

1. 1215: ____

   ____

KEY STRUCTURES: For each key structure, provide a 1-3 sentence summary of how each changed, experienced alteration, or encountered difficulty.

1. Government: ____

   ____

   ____

2. Religion: ____

   ____

   ____

3. Society: ____

   ____

   ____

   ____

COMPREHENSION QUESTIONS: Answer each question as prompted; typical answers should range from 3-8 sentences, depending on the detail of the question.

1. What factors caused such an age of disillusionment in religion among the people of Europe?

2. In Pope Innocent III's eyes, what was needed to fix the age of disillusion?

3. What reforms were impressed upon the priests? How did the bishops respond to these commands of reforms?

4. How did Innocent III handle apathetic bishops? How did he respond to rulers who did not conform to doctrine?

5. How did Innocent III view the Holy Roman Empire and its purpose and relation to the papacy? Summarize the outcome of his dealings as well.

6. Explain the origin and results of the Fourth Crusade.

7. For Innocent III, what factors had brought about such immorality in his age?

8. Explain the origins and result of the Albigensian Crusade.

9. What was the goal of the fourth Lateran Council? How did it seek to achieve its goal?

10. Explain the real meaning of Innocent's claim to "possess the throne of glory"?

11. Summarize the beliefs and lifestyle of the Franciscans.

12. Explain the origins of St. Francis and how he came to commit himself to his mission.

13. What was the difference between St. Francis' and Cardinal Ugolino's view on how to handle the growth of the Franciscan Order?

____

____

____

____

____

____

____

____

____

____

14. At the end of the chapter, what was the state of the Franciscan Order?

____

____

____

____

____

SHORT ANSWER ESSAY QUESTIONS: Provide a short response in the range of 5-8 sentences.
In light of the lives of St. Francis and Ugolino, is it worth compromising your ideals to achieve practical results? Explain why or why not.

____

____

____

____

____

____

____

____

____

____

____

____

____

____

CHAPTER 8
The New Era in Monarchy

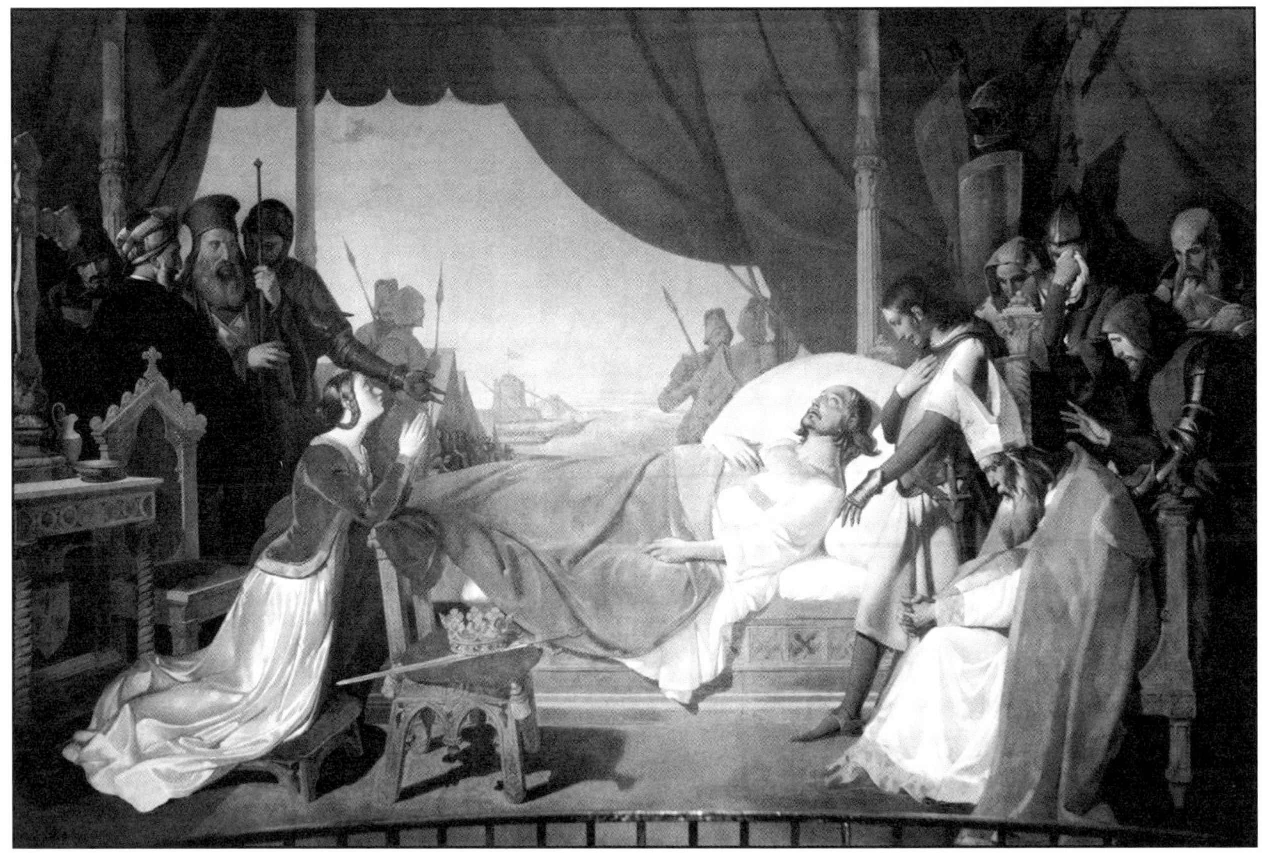

The Death of Saint Louis, French School, Nineteenth Century

INTRODUCTION

Summative Statement: Provide a 1-2 sentence summary/main idea of the entire chapter.

Summative Quote

"Into your hands God has put the kingdom; the affairs of the Church He has committed to us (bishops). ... We are not permitted to exercise an earthly rule; and you, Sire, are not authorized to burn incense." —Hosius of Cordova, regarding the conversion of Constantine[1]

Hook

Have the words of Hosius of Cordova been followed so far in medieval history? Why or why not?

---

1 *A History of Medieval Europe: From Constantine to Saint Louis*, p. 425

KEY TERMS: For each term, provide a 1-2 sentence definition.

1. Treaty of Paris (1259): ____

____

____

____

KEY FIGURES: For each figure, provide a 1-2 sentence definition; make sure to include the person's relevance and major actions in the chapter.

1. Frederick II: ____

____

____

2. Gregory IX: ____

____

____

3. Louis IX: ____

____

____

____

KEY DATES: For each date, find and <u>briefly</u> explain what happened on that date.

1. **1226: ____

____

KEY STRUCTURES: For each key structure, provide a 1-3 sentence summary of how each changed, experienced alteration, or encountered difficulty.

1. Government:____

____

____

____

2. Religion: ____

____

____

3. Society: ____

____

____

COMPREHENSION QUESTIONS: Answer each question as prompted; typical answers should range from 3-8 sentences, depending on the detail of the question.

1. Describe the Norman kingdom of Sicily at the time Frederick II came to power.

2. Explain the origin and purpose of the University of Naples.

3. What did Frederick agree to do in return for Pope Honorius III's support of imperial power?

4. Why did Gregory IX seek to end the alliance between the empire and papacy?

5. To whom did Gregory IX turn for support against the empire? What was the outcome of the new imperial-papal war?

6. How did Louis IX's character earn him the trust of his vassals? Provide at least one specific example.

7. Provide examples of Louis IX's religious fervor.

____

____

____

____

8. Outline the legacy of Louis IX's rule.

____

____

____

____

____

____

____

____

____

SHORT ANSWER ESSAY QUESTIONS: Provide a short response in the range of 5-8 sentences.

In light of the lives of Louis IX and Frederick II, what makes a ruler just? Are there any qualities to Frederick II that made him just? Are there any qualities to Louis IX that made him just? Argue whether or not Frederick II was a more just ruler than Louis IX.

____

____

____

____

____

____

____

____

____

____

____

____

____

____

SUMMATIVE TIMELINE: Continue your summative timeline.

CHAPTER 9
Europe in the Middle of the Thirteenth Century: An Economic Survey

Merchants from Holland and the Middle East Trading in a Mediterranean Port by Thomas Wyck (date unknown)

INTRODUCTION
Summative Statement: Provide a 1-2 sentence summary/main idea of the entire chapter.

Summative Quote

"But man has almost constant occasion for the help of his brethren, and it is in vain for him to expect it from their benevolence only. He will be more likely to prevail if he can interest their self-love in his favour, and shew them that it is for their own advantage to do for him what he requires of them. Whoever offers to another a bargain of any kind, proposes to do this. Give me that which I want, and you shall have this which you want, is the meaning of every such offer; and it is in this manner that we obtain from one another the far greater part of those good offices which we stand in need of. It is not from the benevolence of the butcher, the brewer, or the baker that we expect our dinner, but from their regard to their own interest. We address ourselves, not to their humanity, but to their self-love, and never talk to them of our own necessities, but of their advantages. Nobody but a beggar chooses to depend chiefly upon the benevolence of his fellow-citizens." —The Wealth of Nations, Adam Smith, 1776

Hook
Summarize the main idea of Adam Smith's statement above.

KEY TERMS: For each term, provide a 1-2 sentence definition.

1. "Blue-nails": ____

   ____

2. Fairs of Champagne: _______________________________________

   ____

   ____

   ____

COMPREHENSION QUESTIONS: Answer each question as prompted; typical answers should range from 3-8 sentences, depending on the detail of the question.

1. Outline the state of the Islamic and Byzantine economies by the thirteenth century.

2. Outline the traits and characteristics of a medieval town or commune.

3. Summarize the workings of the cloth industry in northern Europe.

4. Delineate the workings of the spice trade in the Mediterranean.

5. How did Italian businessmen lessen the possibility of loss due to piracy, war, and weather?

6. What are some examples of the mobility of the European population at this time?

7. Outline how Western Europeans were attracted to help colonize the lands east of the Elbe.

8. How did the agricultural revolution in the East help fuel the growth of capitalism in the West?